Learning Short-take®

CONFIDENT FACILITATION SKILLS

Tools and techniques for the professional facilitator

CATHERINE MATTISKE

TPC - The Performance Company Pty Ltd
Level 20, Darling Park
Tower 2, 201 Sussex Street,
Sydney NSW 2000
Australia

ACN 077 455 273
email: tpc@tpc.net.au
Website: www.catherinemattiske.com

© TPC – The Performance Company Pty Limited
First edition published in 2006
Second edition published in 2011
Third edition published in 2022

All rights reserved. Apart from any fair dealing for the purposes of study, research or review, as permitted under Australian copyright law, no part of this publication may be reproduced by any means without the written permission of the copyright owner. Every effort has been made to obtain permission relating to information reproduced in this publication.

The information in this publication is based on the current state of commercial and industry practice, applicable legislation, general law and the general circumstances as at the date of publication. No person shall rely on any of the contents of this publication and the publisher and the author expressly exclude all liability for direct and indirect loss suffered by any person resulting in any way from the use of or reliance on this publication or any part of it. Any options and advice are offered solely in pursuance of the author's and the publisher's intention to provide information, and have not been specifically sought.

For eBook version: By payment of the required fees, you have been granted the non-exclusive, non-transferable right to access and read the text of this e-book on screen. No part of this text may be reproduced, transmitted, downloaded, decompiled, reverse engineered, or stored in or introduced into any information storage retrieval system, in any form or by any means, whether the electronic or mechanical, now known or hereinafter invented, without the express permission of the author.

A catalogue record for this book is available from the National Library of Australia

National Library of Australia
Cataloguing-in-Publication data

Mattiske, Catherine
Confident Facilitation Skills: Tools and Techniques for the Professional Facilitator

ISBN 978-1-921547-05-8

1. Occupational training 2. Learning I. Title

370.113
_____

Distributed by TPC - The Performance Company - www.catherinemattiske.com
For further information contact TPC - The Performance Company, Sydney Australia on +61 (02) 9555 1953.

HELLO.

Welcome to the Learning Short-take® process!

This Learning Short-take® is a bite sized learning package that aims to improve your skills and provide you with an opportunity for personal and professional development to achieve success in your role.

This Learning Short-take® combines self study with workplace activities in a unique learning system to keep you motivated and energized. So let's get started!

Step 1:
What's inside?

- Learning Short-take®. This section contains all of the learning content and will guide you through the learning process.
- Learning Activities. You will be prompted to complete these as you read through.
- Learning Journal. This is a summary of your key learnings. Update it when prompted.
- Skill Development Action Plan. Learning is about taking action. This is your action plan where you'll plan how you will implement your learning.

Step 2:
Complete the Learning Short-take®

- Learning Short-takes® are best completed in a quiet environment that is free of distractions.
- Schedule time in your calendar to complete the Learning Short-take® and prioritize this time as an investment in your own professional development.
- Depending on the title, most participants complete the Learning Short-take® from 90 minutes to 2.5 hours.

Step 3:
Meet with your Manager/Coach

- Schedule a 30 minute meeting with your Manager or Coach.
- At this meeting share your completed Activities, Learning Journal and Skill Development Action Plan.
- Most importantly, discuss and agree on how you will implement your learning in your role.

GET VIP ACCESS TO YOUR MATERIALS

This Learning Short-take® includes an interactive activity book, associated tools and job aids, plus a bonus eBook.

1 Visit https://www.catherinemattiske.com/books

2 Select your book

3 Click: VIP ACCESS

4 Enter the code: CFS2022088

WELCOME

Confident Facilitation Skills
Tools and Techniques for the Professional Facilitator

Confident Facilitation Skills combines self-study with realistic workplace activities to provide you with the key skills and techniques to become a more effective facilitator. You will be guided through a comprehensive approach to prepare for a facilitation session, focus the group, draw out ideas, manage difficult behavior, build consensus, maintain high energy, close the session, and construct customized agendas. **Confident Facilitation Skills** also includes a comprehensive reference guide of proven group facilitation techniques.

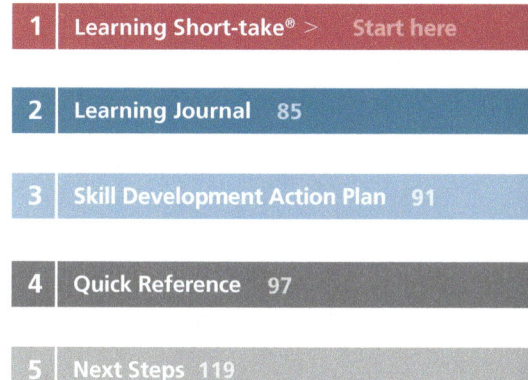

Facilitation is fast becoming a key skill for anyone who is in a team, leading a project team, heading up a working group, or managing a department. Facilitation is the skill and art of guiding others to solve problems to achieve objectives without personally giving advice or offering solutions. A facilitator provides the structure and process - enabling groups to function effectively and make high-quality decisions.

Confident Facilitation Skills includes the **Confident Facilitation Initial Meeting Planning Tool**, provided to you as a free download.

Now let's get started!

"No man is an island, entire of itself; every man is a piece of the continent."

JOHN DONNE

Section 1

LEARNING SHORT-TAKE®

WHAT'S IN THIS LEARNING SHORT-TAKE®

Table of Contents

How to Complete Your Learning Short-take®	5
Activity Checklist	6
Learning Objectives	7
Let's Get Started	8
Part 1 - Getting Started	9
Fundamentals of Facilitation	10
Facilitation Skills	19
Part 2 - Preparing for Facilitation	23
Preparing a Facilitated Session	24
Step 1 - Meet with the Client	25
Step 2 - Design the Session	28
Step 3 - Design the Environment	31
Step 4 - Invite Participants	37
Part 3 - Conducting the Session	39
Beginning the Session	40
The Facilitation Model	49
Questions, Paraphrasing and Summarizing	63
Part 4 - Dealing with Difficult Situations	65
Working with Difficult Attendees	66
Part 5 - Problem Solving Techniques	69
Reference: Problem Solving Techniques	70

© 2022, TPC - The Performance Company Pty Limited. All rights reserved.

HOW TO COMPLETE YOUR LEARNING SHORT-TAKE®

1. **Reflect on your skills and abilities** in facilitation, and how you use this information to improve effectiveness in your role.
2. **Complete the Activities as directed.**
3. **Highlight specific skill areas** that you believe you could develop more. Add these to the **Learning Journal.** Add to your Learning Journal as you go.
4. When you have completed this Learning Short-take® **meet with your Manager/Coach.** In this meeting, you will jointly establish a personal Skills Development Action Plan.
5. **Subject to your coach's final review** and assessment, you will either sign off the module, or undertake further skill development as appropriate.

ACTIVITY CHECKLIST

During this Learning Short-take® you will be prompted to complete the following activities:

- Activity 1 - Facilitator Assignments   17
- Activity 2 - Initial Skills Self-Assessment   20
- Activity 3 - Welcome Elements   38
- Activity 4 - Facilitating Conflict   47
- Activity 5 - Facilitation Model   61
- Learning Journal   85
- Skill Development Action Plan   91

LEARNING OBJECTIVES

By the end of this Learning Short-take® participants should be able to:

- Define the role of a facilitator.
- Identify the key facilitation principles.
- Describe best practices related to each facilitation principle.
- Differentiate between process and content facilitation.
- Identify the core practices and skills required for effective facilitation.
- Explain how to stimulate group participation and positively handle conflict.
- Create a Skill Development Action Plan.

"Attitude is a little thing that makes a big difference."

WINSTON CHURCHILL

LET'S GET STARTED

Facilitation is fast becoming a key skill for anyone who is in a team, leading a project team, heading up a working group or managing a department. Facilitation is the skill, and art of guiding others to solve problems and achieve objectives without personally giving advice or offering solutions. A facilitator provides the structure and process - enabling groups to function effectively and make high-quality decisions.

This Learning Short-take® combines self-study with workplace activities to provide you with the key skills and techniques to become an effective facilitator. You will learn how to motivate and enable groups to develop team plans and provide solutions to team problems. You will be guided through a comprehensive approach to prepare for a facilitation session, focus the group, use (not abuse) the power of the pen, gather information, manage dysfunction, build consensus, maintain high energy, close the session, and construct customized agendas. The Learning Short-take® is designed for completion in approximately 90 minutes.

GETTING STARTED

PART 1

FUNDAMENTALS OF FACILITATION

The term facilitation has broad meaning. In the context of this Learning Short-take®, facilitation refers to leading and guiding a group, without bias, to discover insights and reach an intended outcome.

Facilitation of group discussion is a technique that encourages the group to express and discuss their own ideas. The group is the reservoir of knowledge and creativity; the facilitator "serves" the group by building trust, remaining neutral, and not evaluating or contributing his or her own ideas.

The role of Facilitator defined

The role of the facilitator is to encourage discussion, help clarify when necessary, and assist the group in summarizing their ideas. The facilitator is concerned with the process – what is going on in the group; they do not control the content. Facilitation requires skill in questioning, paraphrasing, and summarizing. It also demands careful attention to group dynamics. The facilitator may need to encourage quiet participants, move the conversation away from dominant participants, and deal with disruptive participants.

There are no prescribed rules for good facilitation, however there are tips and tricks to promote success. In addition to sound facilitation skills, each facilitation situation depends on the facilitator's personality, the circumstances, and the nature of the people in the group.

"We all arrived and sat in a meeting. What made this meeting different from all the others we'd attended was that our manager introduced a person whose role was to facilitate our meeting. After seeing the meeting begin and end on time and the purpose of the meeting actually accomplished, our group thought, "So that's what facilitation is all about, someone runs a meeting for us."

What didn't they see?

- That they could converse and accomplish their purpose faster.
- That they shared more ideas and knowledge.
- That their results were of a higher quality because everyone in the group had equal opportunity to contribute.
- That people in their group with differing viewpoints had their ideas married together.
- That everyone left in agreement and with a common understanding of what had occurred and what was to happen next.

Excellence in facilitation often goes unnoticed and is simply a process for achieving the objectives of a meeting in a very subtle way.

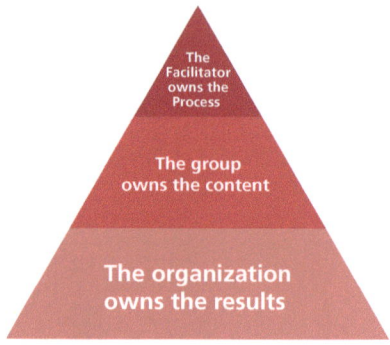

The Facilitator vs. Group Relationship

The group should do most of the talking. Facilitators need to be aware of how much they talk. They should not be dominating the conversation, or be a focal point of the conversation.

The diagrams below show the difference between controlling and facilitating a conversation.

Leader-centered:
- Introduce new ideas
- Lead through series of steps
- Test knowledge
- Review activity

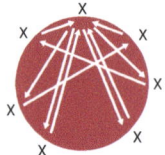

Facilitator:
- Help group process own ideas
- Knowledge resides in group
- Manage process, not content
- Encourages all to participate

Facilitators need to be able to tolerate silence. Silence can mean various things: lack of understanding of a question or of the process, confusion, thinking or reflecting, or needing time to translate ideas and language.

Traits of an Excellent Facilitator

A facilitator is many things:

- An internal or external person who designs work sessions with a specific focus or intent.
- An advisor who brings out the full potential of a working group.
- A provider of processes, tools and techniques to get work accomplished effectively and efficiently in a group environment.
- A person who keeps a group meeting on track.
- Someone who helps resolve conflict.
- Someone who draws out participation from everyone.
- Someone who organizes the work of a group.
- Someone who makes sure that the goals are met.
- Someone who provides structure to the work of a group.

"A penny will hide the biggest star in the Universe if you hold it close enough to your eye."

SAMUEL GRAFTON

> *"If the only tool you have is a hammer, you tend to see every problem as a nail."*
>
> ABRAHAM MASLOW

What a Facilitator Isn't

Facilitation is not:

- Training.
- Meeting Management.
- One-on-one Coaching.
- Group therapy.
- Changing the input/words of participants to suit themselves.
- Refusing to record an idea.
- Getting involved in the content of the group.
- Fixing the group.
- Fixing the problem for the group.
- Attaching to outcomes.
- Judging comments of the group, liking some ideas better than others.
- Mixing up the agenda and or work processes.
- Manipulating people and behaviors through their own feedback.
- Monopolizing conversation.
- Taking sides on issues or people.
- Being closed to group suggestions on the process.
- Trying to have all the answers.

Choosing an Internal vs. External Facilitator

Outlined below are three options for handling facilitation:

1. **Use an Internal Facilitator.** Using an internal facilitator saves time and complexity of introducing an outsider to the organization. It also provides one or more employees the opportunity to exercise facilitation skills, makes good use of the organization's resources, and helps to foster internal commitment to project process and outcomes. However, the facilitator must be objective and neutral throughout the process and this is often a challenge for internal resources.

2. **Hire an External Facilitator.** Engaging a qualified outside volunteer or paid consultant brings expertise to the role, frees internal resources to focus on the process, and provides a catalyst for keeping on track. However, it is important that an outside facilitator be somewhat familiar with the content being discussed and is a quick study with regard to an organizational background and culture. Bringing in an outside facilitator is one way of demonstrating commitment to the topic at hand, and because of the outsider's neutrality, participants may find it easier to be honest.

3. **Do not assign a facilitator.**
   This option is most effective for experienced organizations or those who have a strong commitment to developing shared skills in meeting and process management. Without a facilitator, it is especially important that groups have ground rules for their work and guard against irrelevant discussion, individuals who dominate, and any dissent among group members.

Complete Activity # 1
Facilitator Assignments

ACTIVITY 1: FACILITATOR ASSIGNMENTS

Look at the following business interactions. Circle or highlight those which you consider to be appropriate for a facilitator:

- A coaching session
- A communications / liaison meeting
- A conflict amongst two employees
- A performance review
- A focus group to gather input on a new program or product
- A priority-setting meeting
- A meeting to negotiate team roles and responsibilities
- A problem solving meeting
- A meeting to share feedback and improve performance
- A meeting where the facilitators opinion is sought
- A training workshop
- A program review / evaluation process
- A team building session
- A session to clarify objectives and create detailed results indicators
- A strategic planning session

Activity #1 - check your answers

Check your work from the previous activity.
The following highlighted interactions are typical facilitator assignments.

A coaching session
A priority-setting meeting
A team building session
A performance review
A problem solving meeting
A meeting to share feedback and improve performance
A session to clarify objectives and create detailed results indicators
A conflict amongst two employees
A training workshop
A program review / evaluation process
A communications / liaison meeting
A focus group to gather input on a new program or product
A strategic planning session
A meeting where the facilitators opinion is sought
A meeting to negotiate team roles and responsibilities

Now update your Learning Journal (page 85)

FACILITATION SKILLS

Are You A Facilitator?

Here are a few questions to help you answer that question. Your honest answers will help you determine whether or not you would be comfortable facilitating.

1. Are you willing to listen to others without judgment or preconceived notions about what they should or shouldn't say or do?	Yes ☐ No ☐
2. Do you show respect for the opinions of others even when they disagree with you?	Yes ☐ No ☐
3. Can you release the need to have complete control of a conversation or other situations?	Yes ☐ No ☐
4. Are you comfortable dealing with conflict?	Yes ☐ No ☐
5. Are you comfortable speaking in public?	Yes ☐ No ☐
6. Are you able to laugh at yourself?	Yes ☐ No ☐
7. Can you think on your feet?	Yes ☐ No ☐
8. Do you believe that groups working together are smarter than individuals working alone?	Yes ☐ No ☐
9. Can you accept feedback from others about yourself?	Yes ☐ No ☐

Answering yes to a majority of these questions indicates that you would be comfortable in the role of facilitator.

Reflect on your answers to this activity. Before reading on, establish where you think your current level of facilitation skills are.

Facilitation Skill Levels

The following four levels will assist in determining your current facilitation skills and areas for development.

Level 1

Understanding concepts; values and beliefs; use of facilitative behaviors such as active listening, paraphrasing, questioning, summarizing; managing time; encouraging participation; keeping clear and accurate notes; using basic tools like problem solving and action planning.

Level 2

Mastering process tools; designing meetings; skilled at using the right decision-making method, achieving consensus, and getting true closure; handling feedback activities and conducting process checks; using exit surveys; good at managing meetings in an effective manner; able to help a group set goals and objectives that are measurable; skilled at checking assumptions and challenging ideas.

Level 3

Skilled at managing conflict and making immediate interventions; able to deal with resistance and personal attacks; making design changes on the spot; sizing up a group and using the right strategies for its developmental stage; managing feedback activities; able to design facilitation sessions; consolidating ideas from a mass of information into coherent summaries.

Level 4

Design and implement process interventions in response to complex organizational issues; use tools to promote process improvement, customer intimacy and overall organizational effectiveness; able to support teams in the various stages of team development.

Complete Activity # 2
Initial Skills Self-Assessment

ACTIVITY 2: INITIAL SKILLS SELF-ASSESSMENT

Rate yourself on each of the techniques.
7 is competent and confident, little need for improvement
4 is average, needs improvement
1 is uncomfortable, major need for improvement
- Note specific areas of improvement related to each skill that you would like to develop. Be sure to include your *reasons* for your rating in each skill.
- Start thinking about a personal development plan and identify two or three things you could do to improve your skills in this area and write them in the space provided.

I…	Rating	Reasoning
Level 1 Concepts, values and beliefs		
understand the concepts, values and beliefs of facilitation.	1 2 3 4 5 6 7	
am skilled at active listening, paraphrasing, questioning and summarizing key points.	1 2 3 4 5 6 7	
am able to manage time and maintain a good pace.	1 2 3 4 5 6 7	
am armed with techniques for getting active participation and generating ideas.	1 2 3 4 5 6 7	
keep clear and accurate notes that reflect what participants have said.	1 2 3 4 5 6 7	
am familiar with the basic tools of systematic problem solving, brainstorming and force-field analysis (cause and effect diagram).	1 2 3 4 5 6 7	
Level 2 Process tools, designing meetings		
have knowledge of a wide range of procedural tools essential for structuring group discussions.	1 2 3 4 5 6 7	
am able to design meetings using a broad set of process tools.	1 2 3 4 5 6 7	
have knowledge of decision making processes.	1 2 3 4 5 6 7	
am skilled at achieving consensus and gaining closure.	1 2 3 4 5 6 7	
am skilled at using the feedback process. Able to hear and accept personal feedback.	1 2 3 4 5 6 7	
am able to set goals and objectives that are measurable.	1 2 3 4 5 6 7	
am able to ask good probing questions that challenge my own and others assumptions in a non-threatening way.	1 2 3 4 5 6 7	

© 2022, TPC - The Performance Company Pty Limited. All rights reserved.

ACTIVITY 2: CONTINUED

I...	Rating	Reasoning
am able to stop the action and check on how things are going.	1 2 3 4 5 6 7	
am able to use evaluation to improve facilitation sessions.	1 2 3 4 5 6 7	
am able to manage meetings in an orderly and effective manner.	1 2 3 4 5 6 7	
Level 3 Managing conflict and interventions		
am able to manage conflict between participants and remain composed.	1 2 3 4 5 6 7	
am able to make quick and effective interventions.	1 2 3 4 5 6 7	
am able to deal with resistance non-defensively.	1 2 3 4 5 6 7	
am skilled at dealing with personal attacks.	1 2 3 4 5 6 7	
am able to redesign meeting processes on the spot.	1 2 3 4 5 6 7	
am able to size up a group and use the right strategies for their developmental stage.	1 2 3 4 5 6 7	
am able to implement feedback processes.	1 2 3 4 5 6 7	
am able to integrate and consolidate ideas from a mass of information and create coherent summaries.	1 2 3 4 5 6 7	
Level 4 Design and implement process interventions		
am able to design and implement process interventions in response to complex organizational issues.	1 2 3 4 5 6 7	
am able to facilitate process improvement interventions in response to complex organizational issues.	1 2 3 4 5 6 7	
am able to support teams in all stages of their development.	1 2 3 4 5 6 7	

Personal development plan ideas:

1

2

Now update your Learning Journal (page 85)

PREPARING FOR FACILITATION

PART 2

PREPARING A FACILITATED SESSION

The key to successful facilitation is planning and preparation. Your design will provide a framework or a structure that will optimize the participants' time together, allow a way for people to talk to each other constructively, and produce the desired results of the meeting.

Session design includes:

1. **Meeting with your Client** to determine the essence or purpose of the facilitation.
2. **Designing the Session**.
3. **Designing the Environment** in which the group will work.
4. **Inviting the Participants**

How you approach design will vary with your own personal style and experience as well as the complexity of the session you're facilitating. An advanced facilitator may feel comfortable going through the entire design process with the client during the initial interview. Those less experienced may need to do the work process design after the interview and then finalize it in a follow-on meeting.

STEP 1 - MEET WITH THE CLIENT

Regardless of whether you are an internal or external client you should meet with the person who has requested you as a facilitator. An initial meeting with your client is very important for both of you. It gives each of you the opportunity to get acquainted as well as to explore the reasons for the facilitation. Be aware that the client will be evaluating you and will determine how much to trust you. The more relaxed and confident you are, the deeper the level of trust that can develop between you.

Anyone acting as a facilitator must be very clear about their own beliefs. Our assumptions about organizations determine, in subtle ways, our own facilitation style and the skills with which we work. For example, if you think your client's employee problems may be solved by enabling a more participative and collaborative group, then you must demonstrate collaboration and participation more with your client.

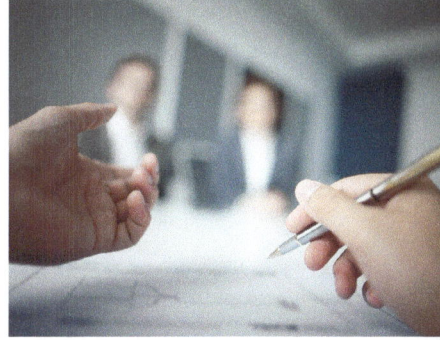

"Is the glass half empty, half full, or twice as large as it needs to be?"

AUTHOR UNKNOWN

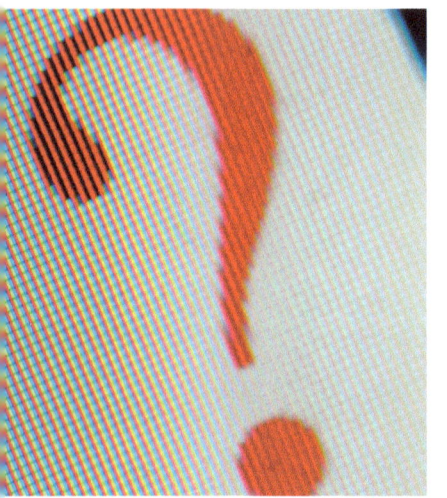

The Essential Questions

1. What is the *goal*?

Goals are typically general in nature. You might like to think of goals as things that can't be measured.

An example would be your client wanting his or her employees to operate like a team instead of the current 'us' and 'them' style that they are using. Your client might describe the desired goal as, "I want everyone working together like one big happy family."

2. What are the *objectives or deliverables* for the meeting?

The objectives or deliverables your client asks for are more tangible and measurable than outcomes.

Using the previous example this might include a vision statement or plan of action, role clarification, written expectations each member has of the group, or a team action plan with responsibilities documented.

Until you obtain clear answers to these questions, designing the session is impossible.

After you and the client have come to an understanding of what each of you need and expect from the other, work process design begins.

TPC Facilitation - Initial Meeting Planning Tool

FREE DOWNLOAD

To download this tool go to **www.catherinemattiske.com/books** and follow the online instructions.

STEP 2 - DESIGN THE SESSION

Designing a session is a learned art. You need a solid knowledge of group dynamics and available tools and techniques in order to do it. Experience also plays an important role in becoming a good designer. Here are the basic steps to follow in the session design process.

1. Clarify the **purpose of the meeting**.
2. Define the desired **goals** and **objectives**.
3. Determine **who should attend**.
4. **Design the sequence of meeting activities**.
   a. List all of the content areas to be covered in the session.
   b. Choose a method of presenting each content area.
   c. Review and adjust your design by asking:
      - Can I get from one step to the next smoothly?
      - Are all steps necessary?
      - How much time will it take?
      - Will these methods work for this group?
      - Is there anything about this method or topic that could blow up?
5. Decide **how to begin and how to conclude** the session.
6. Determine **logistics, equipment and administrative needs**.
7. Complete the **agenda**.
8. **Finalize the design** with your client.

During work process design, keep these factors in mind:

Meeting approach

Is the meeting to be conducted in-person or virtually, using digital meeting and collaboration software? The answer to this question affects the best facilitation approaches to use.

Group size

Groups of ten to twelve may not need to be broken into smaller groups for simple sessions, such as idea generation or dialogue.

Virtual meeting software changes the rules on group size, allowing much larger groups to take on activities than aren't possible in a manual facilitation. This also allows for quick movement in and out of virtual breakouts, if work in small groups is necessary.

Gathering lots of information

When you're hosting multiple sessions that produce large amounts of information, schedule a day or two in between sessions so that you can manage the outputs of each one and prepare properly for the next.

"Whenever you fall, pick something up."

OSWALD AVERY

Use positive words

Frequently, clients request a number of objectives and deliverables for one session. We recommend you describe a session that's going to produce a variety of products as one having an ambitious agenda. Comments to the group like 'We have a lot of work to do today' or 'This is going to be a full day' are discouraging and set the session up as one of drudgery. Negative comments like this will drain participants' energy before they begin.

Post-session completion

Post-session work is not the job of the facilitator. Advise your client in session design of the following:

1. For your session to have lasting impact, each participant may need to receive the documented deliverables of the session as soon as possible.
2. Ensure any follow-up actions, including the completed session documentation, has been assigned before the session ends.
Ask the client to appoint a coordinator.
3. If outputs include a task list or actions, make sure a group member's name and contact details placed on this work.
This allows the member to be contacted if clarification is needed.

STEP 3 - DESIGN THE ENVIRONMENT

The planning stage of a facilitation must also consider the requirements for space, equipment and support. Requirements will be determined by whether the meeting is to be conducted in-person or virtually.

The Physical Meeting Room

Work with your client to secure an appropriate meeting room. We suggest you discuss the following with your client to ensure a suitable environment.

Atmosphere	Is the room a cheerful color and does it have outside windows?
Layout	Is the room large enough for your needs? Will everyone be able to see the resources you work with and each other?
Furniture	Are the chairs comfortable for longer meetings?
Conveniences	How far away are the rest rooms, lunchroom, elevators, and food?
Lighting	Is there sufficient lighting? Can the room be darkened easily?
Noise	Is the room free of excessive noise and interruptions? Will everyone be able to hear what's going on?
Outlets	Are there enough outlets for equipment?
Heat & Cooling	Will the temperature be appropriate and can you control it yourself?

The Virtual Meeting Room

If the meeting is virtual, choose meeting software that is easy to join, has reliable audio, video and screen sharing capabilities, with all functions and features required for the group to discuss, collaborate and, if necessary, break-out into smaller groups.

Consider meeting software such as Zoom, MS Teams, WebEx or Google-Meet in combination with virtual collaboration and whiteboarding tools such as Jamboards or MIRO.

"My play was a complete success. The audience was a failure."

ASHLEIGH BRILLIANT

Plan and Prepare Ahead

Plan the session early enough to ensure the best facilities and set-up. If possible, visit the room, or test the virtual space, before the session and make necessary adjustments. One of the most important things is for everyone to be able to see and hear everything that's going on.

The room (whether physical or virtual) should support good display of your visuals and materials. Make sure that:

1) the contents of any slides or visuals displayed are large and clear enough for everyone to see easily.

2) the lighting and display in the room/ virtual space is suitable for everyone to clearly see each other and the resources you're working with.

3) if using flip chart or other materials in a physical room, there is plenty of wall space to display everything completed during the session.

4) if using a virtual space, digital whiteboards and collaboration tools are good to display information and work together.

In-Person Equipment Checklist (customize as appropriate)

- Flip chart easels
- Extension cords and power strips
- Projection or display screen
- Player or device with speakers for music
- DVD player or screen to display video
- Whiteboard
- Computers or laptops, if required
- Printers
- Extra tables for equipment, materials, group breakout areas
- A refreshments table in the room providing light snacks and drinks

Logistics Checklist

- Blank paper
- Extra flip chart paper
- Folders
- Big marker pens (lots of colors)
- Masking and transparent tape
- Pencils and pens
- Scissors
- Stapler
- Whiteboard markers and erasers
- Large self-sticking notes for all the participants
- Other requirements
    - A person to record the session
    - Transportation/travel arrangements for participants if necessary

In-Person Room Layout

There are several choices for setting up the room for optimum communication. Room layout sets up participant expectations for the meeting and can create a more comfortable, relaxed feeling among attendees. Clustered seating encourages collaborative interactions among group members.

- U-Shape: Form tables in a U-shape with chairs on the outside. The open part of the U is for presentation.
- Semicircle: The U-shape for smaller groups. Place a flip chart on an easel in the open end of the semicircle.
- Round Table: If there will be a lot of writing, use a large round table. Leave a space open at the table for presentation materials. This also works well if the facilitator will be seated.
- Herringbone: This is a variation you can use when you need a U-shape and there isn't room. Arrange two sets of tables in a herringbone shape with chairs on the outside only. The facilitator and equipment can face these two tables.
- Elevated, stair-stepped, U-Shape: Virtual meeting facilities for large groups are often arranged in this auditorium style with the workstations arranged along raised, curved rows. The facilitator is in the front at the lowest level with sophisticated projection or display systems.
  The deviation of the U-shape is successful because the virtual meeting process and software tools enliven the attention and participation of the group.
- Rows: This layout isn't conducive to facilitated meetings as people can't see everyone else in the room and collaboration is difficult. Consider moving the chairs into a semicircle or move the chairs completely away from the tables.

Using Technology to assist facilitation

New technology is being released at lightening speed. Ensure you keep up to date with what's new on the market. The following types of technology are worth evaluating for use during an in-person or virtual process:

- **Smart boards:** The contents of a white board are either printed directly from the board or are inserted into graphics software.

- **Pen-based or Touchscreen technology:** A touchscreen, or the pen you use on a projection screen or digital whiteboard is software smart and is a fast, convenient way to write, interact and send comments.

- **Modeling software:** Software tools that graphically depict modeling work produced in session.

- **Digital meeting systems:** Virtual meeting software, collaboration tools, or projection systems that automate, capture and improve the basic set of facilitated functions such as brainstorming, editing, categorizing, generating lists and ideas, providing background documents and voting.

Like all facilitation methods, benefits depend on what it is you're trying to accomplish and who your participants are. If you're considering the use of digital or automated tools in your session, please consider the following trade-offs.

Benefits of New Technology

- Can speed up the session and keep things neat and organized.
- Participants leave with their own copy of session products.
- Allows bigger than flip chart paper or single-screen products like matrices, workflows or models.
- Can reduce or eliminate post-session work.
- Can get to the final product quicker, often before the end of the session.

Disadvantages of New Technology

- May distract participants if used inappropriately.
- May intimidate participants, depending on their background.
- Can change the tone and focus of the group.
- Requires a software or technical expert and associated equipment.
- Costs of technology may outweigh traditional methods such as flipcharts etc.

STEP 4 - INVITE PARTICIPANTS

An important step is to notify the participants of the session two to three weeks prior to the scheduled date. The notification should clearly articulate who the Leader (or sponsor) is, the benefits of the session, when and where the session will be, any pre-work or preparation that is required to be completed, a contact for participants to refer questions to, and a positive reinforcement for participating.

Nexus Resort ~ Nexus Island ~ South Pacific

Meeting Invitation

To: Chris Tyler, Resort Catering Manager
From: Dan Morrison

Dear Chris,

Our VP of Operations, Lyn Jameson has asked that your work team resolve the problem of increased incidences of food poisoning, suspected as a result of the seafood being served in The Pier restaurant. Lyn has asked me to facilitate a series of problem-solving meetings with you, your team and other key employees of Nexus Resort. Separate invitations have been sent to each of your team members.

The benefits of solving this problem are:
- Reduced or eliminated incidents of food poisoning.
- Identification of the source of the problem.
- Opportunity to revise all processes related to the serving of seafood at the resort.
- Increased customer satisfaction.
- Reduced stress for front-line staff.

We will hold the first meeting at 10:00am on Thursday 4th in the Beachcomber Room in the south wing.

Before the meeting, please review the attached documents and be prepared to brainstorm possible solutions. I will be a neutral facilitator during these sessions and my goal is to help the group identify the required action to solve this problem.

Please call me on my Cell/Mobile number if I can answer any questions regarding the meeting objectives or the facilitation process.

Thanks for helping to solve this problem!
Dan

Complete Activity # 3
Welcome Elements

ACTIVITY 3: WELCOME ELEMENTS

Identify the following elements in the sample message below:
1. Who the Leader (or sponsor) is.
2. The benefits of the session.
3. When and where the session will be.
4. Any pre-work that is required to be completed.
5. A contact for participants to refer to with questions.
6. Positive reinforcement for participating.

Nexus Resort ~ Nexus Island ~ South Pacific

Meeting Invitation

To: Chris Tyler, Resort Catering Manager
From: Dan Morrison

Dear Chris,

Our VP of Operations, Lyn Jameson has asked that your work team resolve the problem of increased incidences of food poisoning, suspected as a result of the seafood being served in The Pier restaurant. Lyn has asked me to facilitate a series of problem-solving meetings with you, your team and other key employees of Nexus Resort. Separate invitations have been sent to each of your team members.

The benefits of solving this problem are:
- Reduced or eliminated incidents of food poisoning.
- Identification of the source of the problem.
- Opportunity to revise all processes related to the serving of seafood at the resort.
- Increased customer satisfaction.
- Reduced stress for front-line staff.

We will hold the first meeting at 10:00am on Thursday 4th in the Beachcomber Room in the south wing.

Before the meeting, please review the attached documents and be prepared to brainstorm possible solutions. I will be a neutral facilitator during these sessions and my goal is to help the group identify the required action to solve this problem.

Please call me on my Cell/Mobile number if I can answer any questions regarding the meeting objectives or the facilitation process.

Thanks for helping to solve this problem!
Dan

Now update your Learning Journal (page 85)

CONDUCTING THE SESSION
PART 3

BEGINNING THE SESSION

"Teamwork divides the task and multiplies the success."

AUTHOR UNKNOWN

Whether you are facilitating in-person or virtually, we recommend that before the session begins, you meet and greet participants and chat informally to the group. This simple strategy immediately allays fears (both yours and theirs) and helps to build trust and rapport.

The Opening Flow: Welcome, Icebreaker, Agenda, Ground-rules/Expectations

All sessions need an introduction. The nature of the introduction will depend on the facilitation design and your facilitation style. The introductory segment should always include the actions listed below.

- **Welcome.**
- **Icebreaker** - get the group involved.
- **The Agenda.**
- Develop **Ground Rules** and **Expectations** for the session.

Welcome

Things to include in your welcome are:

- Your name.
- Your role as facilitator, which might include some of the following points:
    - The group is there to talk to each other, not you.
    - The group has the answer and the skills to produce it.
    - You're objective.
    - Your responsibility is to protect the process and keep the session on track.
    - Your job ends at the end of the session.
    - You might have to call "time outs" if the group is wandering.
    - You have a tool kit of techniques to help them work their issues.
    - How your role relates to the client during the session (often their boss).
- The Aim of the session.
- Acknowledge and thank the group for their participation.

"The world is round and the place which may seem like the end may also be only the beginning."

IVY BAKER PRIEST

"Think big thoughts but relish small pleasures."

H. JACKSON BROWN, JR.,
LIFE'S LITTLE INSTRUCTION BOOK

Icebreakers

Beginning a session by going around the room and giving one's name and title can establish barriers of rank in the session. Leave titles out of introductions to set the stage for more democratic participation.

The benefits of a prepared icebreaker are:

1. Introducing participants to the group.
2. Enhancing interpersonal relationships.
3. Relieving anxiety.

Structured activities, even if very casual, help participants get involved more quickly, increase their energy and interest, and help to get them acquainted if they haven't met. If the group already knows each other, have an icebreaker that focuses less on names and more on something unique about the participants in the group i.e. something that was previously unknown about them.

Icebreaker Ideas

Ensure that the icebreaker that you use is appropriate for the level of the group and the culture of your organization.

1. A set of trivia questions may be appropriate, especially if you are going to be doing things that are new to them, like team building or process improvement. The questions can be teaching points later regarding change, innovation, focus, perception and other pertinent content areas. Few people may know the actual answers, so you can make the multiple choice answers amusing to make everyone laugh and feel comfortable.

2. Ask participants to pair up and introduce each other. After a two to three minute interview of each partner, they each introduce the other. This alleviates the tension surrounding introductions as it is much easier to introduce another person than it is yourself. This activity can run virtually using breakouts or paired chat.

3. Participants share three things about themselves one of which is untrue. The whole group guesses which is untrue. This activity can be linked into the session through the themes of new information, change, and accepting everyone's contribution in the group.

You may want to start a collection of ideas as you discover them so that you have a variety to choose from for different types of sessions. There are books available which will give you ideas for Icebreakers. Other facilitators or trainers are also a good source of ideas. Always adapt these activities to fit the facilitation.

"There are no menial jobs, only menial attitudes."

WILLIAM J. BENNETT,
THE BOOK OF VIRTUES

The Agenda

It is always advisable to give the group a prepared agenda as this becomes the road map for working together. Everyone has their own preferred learning style - visual, auditory or kinesthetic (active participation & doing). Providing a visual agenda, as well as speaking to the agenda, ensures people are clear about the session structure.

Don't structure the Agenda with structured times for each session. People who find comfort in clear-cut delineations of time become very uncomfortable if the advertised schedule isn't met. By avoiding exact times for each part of the process, there are no time expectations and no time pressures!

Group Norms

In the introductory part of the session, you will lead the group in developing norms for their behavior. Ground or House Rules are developed by the participants, recorded exactly as they were said, and prominently displayed during the session.

You begin by asking the group to develop the rules under which they will check their behavior during the session. You might ask them the following questions to prompt thinking around effective rules for the group:

1. What behaviors do you feel are important to achieve success for this meeting?
2. What behaviors would you consider to be detrimental to our success?

Facilitators and group members may feel uncomfortable the first time they develop norms. However, groups appreciate having a set of rules to work to and simply generating this list creates a framework of order for the session.

There are several reasons for this.

- If the group works together daily, the list allows everyone to agree on rules for this particular meeting.
- If there have been interpersonal conflicts, this list can suspend fears about conflicts arising during this session.
- If the group doesn't know each other, it allows them to create a framework that can avoid any potentially troublesome personal behaviors.

By establishing ground rules with the group, you should also find that they feel empowered to self-regulate and hold each other accountable to the agreed behaviors.

Example of Ground/House Rules

- Exercise trust, openness, and honesty.
- Focus on solution and resolution.
- Be open to new ways of thinking.
- Honesty is needed to advance our team.
- One conversation at a time.
- No rank in the room.
- Silence is acceptable.
- No "grandstanding".
- Group will follow the process.
- Group will help the facilitator.
- Be on time.
- No rewind.
- Have fun!

If you've developed a theme for the session, it's easy to use the theme as part of group norms. The theme may be about going out into the future so a spaceship theme may be used. The House Rules become "Crew Rules".

Complete Activity # 4
Facilitating Conflict

ACTIVITY 4: FACILITATING CONFLICT

Review the statements and identify which are Healthy Debates vs Dysfunctional Arguments.

- Discussions allow participants to express differences of opinions that lead to a result
- Discussions lead to disaster and breakdown
- Discussions slow down when they look to be coming off track so that participants can resume calm
- Everyone tries to understand the view of the other person
- Extreme anger to the point where relationships are damaged
- Negative body language, like glaring and finger pointing
- Hot topics get thrashed
- Participants assume they are right
- No one is interested in how the other person sees the situation
- Participants "Yeah, butting" and criticizing each other's ideas
- Participants are open to hearing others' ideas
- Participants becoming angry, defensive and personal with each other
- Participants get personally attacked and blamed
- Participants listen and respond to ideas even if they don't agree with them
- Participants stay objective and focus on the facts
- Participants wait until others have finished taking, then state their ideas without responding to ideas of the other person
- Quiet participants "shutting down" to stay out of it
- Sarcastic or dismissive remarks
- There's a systematic approach to analyzing the situation and looking for solutions

Activity #4 - check your answers

Check your work from the previous activity.

Healthy Debates	Dysfunctional Arguments
Participants are open to hearing others' ideas.	Participants assume they are right.
Participants listen and respond to ideas even if they don't agree with them.	Participants wait until others have finished talking, then state their ideas without responding to ideas of the other person.
Everyone tries to understand the view of the other person.	No one is interested in how the other person sees the situation.
Participants stay objective and focus on the facts.	Participants get personally attacked and blamed.
There's a systematic approach to analyzing the situation and looking for solutions.	Hot topics get thrashed.
Discussions allow participants to express differences of opinions that lead to a result.	Discussions lead to disaster and breakdown.
Discussions slow down when they look to be coming off track so that participants can resume calm.	Participants becoming angry, defensive and personal with each other.
	Negative body language, like glaring and finger pointing.
	Sarcastic or dismissive remarks.
	Participants "Yeah, butting" and criticizing each other's ideas.
	Quiet participants "shutting down" to stay out of it.
	Extreme anger to the point where relationships are damaged.

Now update your Learning Journal (page 85)

THE FACILITATION MODEL

The following six-phase model assists a facilitator to confidently to guide the group through the facilitated session:

1. What is the **Issue** the group is trying to address?
2. What are the **Concerns** of each member of the group regarding the issue?
3. What are some **Possibilities** to solve the concerns?
4. What **Criteria** will the group use to judge each possibility?
5. What **Action** items will be selected from the list of possibilities?
6. **Check** to see if the action addresses the issue and the group's concerns.

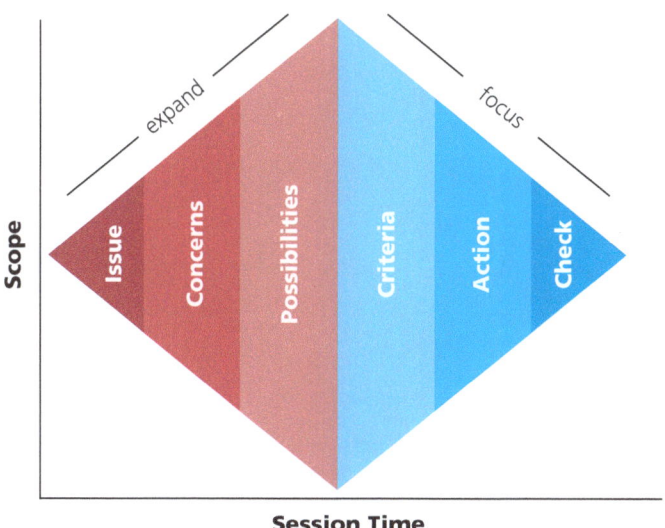

Next, let's deep-dive into each phase.

Phase 1 - Identify the Issue

As a facilitator assume nothing is a given or common knowledge to all participants.

Our Issue is:

We need to create a new way to store and transport fresh fish to avoid further instances of food poisoning amongst resort guests.

Without a clear understanding of the issue the group may move ahead and potentially get no-where or have to retrace their steps and focus on the real issue.

Facilitation process for this phase:

1. Ask the group, "What's the issue?"
2. Record each persons contribution.
3. Find common elements amongst the ideas.
4. Build a draft issue statement. Using common ideas, write a draft issue (beware: don't jump to any solutions).
5. Have group revise issue statement.
6. Ask the group: "Is this the issue?"
7. Ensure the group agrees before continuing. Otherwise return to step 5.
8. Display the agreed Issue Statement clearly.
9. Refer back to the Issue Statement at regular intervals throughout the session.

Phase 2 - Concerns

Its important to gather the concerns from the participants without judgement and without delving into potential negative comments and long-winded discussions.

Facilitation process for this phase:

1. Explain what concerns are. Concerns are personal thoughts, feelings, or reflections.
2. Ask each person for their concerns. Encourage each participant in turn to provide their concerns in one sentence beginning with "I feel…" or "I'm concerned about…"
3. Discourage debate, criticism or challenges from other participants. Reinforce the rule of "no criticism".
4. Be careful not to say "That's good" or "Good thought" but rather "Thank you".
5. After writing up each person's concern, clarify that this is what they have said or mean.
6. If a participant is having difficulty with this step simply say "That's OK… we can come back to you, or you can pass"
7. Display the Concerns clearly
8. Refer back to the Concerns throughout the session where necessary, especially during the Possibilities phase.

Concerns

Our Concerns:

- Publicity
- Problem stopped temporarily.
- Complex process.
- Nervous
- Need to face resort guests every day.
- Supplier contract implications.
- Costs for new process.
- Worried that there won't be an easy fix.

"There's an alternative. There's always a third way, and it's not a combination of the other two ways. It's a different way."

DAVID CARRADINE

Phase 3 - Possible Solutions

Possible solutions are the foundation for new and creative approaches to addressing the issue. Open brainstorming is an easy and highly interactive way for groups to generate innovative answers. Brainstorming can be done in several ways:

- Free Wheeling: Also known as 'Popcorn'. Group members call out ideas.

- Round Robin: where group members take turns contributing one at a time (draws out quieter participants and encourages interaction by all).

- Write and Review Method: Using paper or virtual notes, participants write one idea per note and post onto a wall, flipchart or virtual collaboration space. Facilitator then clusters the ideas into groups and invites further input/clarification as needed.

Facilitation process for this phase:

1. Explain the rules of brainstorming:
   a. One person speaks at a time.
   b. No criticism of other people's ideas.
   c. OK to ask for clarification of an idea.
   d. Building upon ideas is encouraged.

2. Ask each person for their idea or solution. Encourage each participant in turn to provide their idea, concisely and unreservedly; also check whether they are building upon another idea.

3. Discourage debate, criticism or challenges from other participants.

4. If a participant is having difficulty with this step simply say "That's OK… we can come back to you, or you can pass".

5. Ensure that each person's idea or solution is written up, and clarify that this is what they have said or mean.

6. Display the Ideas and Solutions clearly.

7. Refer back to the Ideas throughout the session where necessary, and especially in the Action phase.

Possibilities

Possibilities:

- Investigate fishing boat cold storage.
- Guest survey.
- Kitchen hygiene investigation.
- Survey other customers of fishing fleet to see if problem exists.
- Check all kitchen processes.
- Check other seafood restaurants in area - might not be us.

Phase 4 - Criteria

This step focuses on the rationale for determining action steps necessary to address the issue. This step also helps the group explain at a later date their rationale of why (or why not) the group decided on a specific course of action. Criteria are the filter that possibilities must successfully pass through before becoming action items or recommendations.

Basic Criteria

- Must be legal and moral.
- Must be achievable.
- Must be able to be communicated in an understandable way to others.
- Must meet the needs of the issue.
- Must take resources into consideration.

Advanced Criteria

- Be consistent with the organizations vision and mission (goals).
- Consider the impact on the group and others.
- Be cost effective in relation to the scope of the issue.
- Have an owner and be manageable.
- Have measurable results.
- Meet any contractual obligations.
- Allow for input from key stakeholders and others in the organization.
- Address short-term and long-term implications.
- Be clear focused.
- Have a clear end-point (a life cycle).
- Be able to get customer approval and buy-in.
- Add value.
- Incorporate feedback process.
- Resolve the problem in a timely manner.

Facilitation process for this phase:

1. Use the Basic Criteria and Advanced Criteria lists as resources for suggesting possible criterion to the group.
2. Show some example criteria from a standard list to prompt ideas.
3. List all possible criterion suggested by the group. To prompt the group for ideas use the phrase: "Whatever we do, it will…"
4. Use consensus-building tools to obtain the group's final list.
5. Add specificity to the list to force the group to pinpoint their criteria. Doing so, will greatly help when you use them to eliminate unqualified possibilities.

Criteria

Possible Criteria

- Achievable easily
- Understandable to all
- No impact on budget
- Supports union contract
- Helps me keep my job
- Legal & moral
- Customers are not effected
- Is quick to implement
- Simple
- Fair to everyone
- Does not expose us to the media

Becomes after refinement

Our Criteria

Whatever we do, it will…

- Be easy to implement
- Satisfy the resort guests needs
- Be cost-effective
- Keep current suppliers in place

Adding further specificity

Final Criteria

Whatever we do, it will…

- Be a solution designed and implemented within 4 weeks
- Result 90% on the next customer satisfaction survey in the food quality category.
- Cost less than $150,000
- Keep supplier contractual arrangements for their current contract term.

Phase 5 - Action

In our society we have a tendency to rush into action. Unfortunately many groups rush from Phase 2 - Concerns, to Phase 5 - Actions. Ensure your group takes it's time to work through all Possibilities and Criteria, otherwise back-tracking may be required. The final output of this phase is a list of action items in three components: who, what, when.

Action

Actions

- Consult all contractors
  - Operations Manager
  - Meeting with set criteria for questions regarding on-board cold storage, handling, transportation.
  - Within 7 days
- Guest survey
  - Manager
  - Standard survey
  - Each week for 6 weeks.
- Kitchen hygiene investigation
  - Safety Council
  - Cleanliness/Storage Audit
  - Daily

Facilitation process for this phase:

1. Refer to the group's recorded Possibilities and Final Criteria.
2. For each possibility ask: "Does this possibility satisfy our criteria?"
3. If the group agrees it does not - strike it out.
4. If the group agrees it does - leave it on the list (for now at least).
5. If the group is undecided discuss the criteria further until resolution is achieved.
6. After going through the entire list of possibilities, try to group similar possibilities.
7. Rewrite the remainder into a new list.
8. Build action items for each item - based on "What", "Who", and "When".
9. Check action items against Concerns raised in Phase 2.

Building Consensus - Helpful questions

- Can anyone NOT live with this proposal?
- Does anyone have any heartache with this?
- I just want to get a feel for where we are. Let's take a nonbinding straw vote. How many of you support this…?
- It seems that you can't support this part of the proposal. What do we have to change to make it acceptable to you?
- What would be an acceptable proposal to you?

"Make your optimism come true."

AUTHOR UNKNOWN

Check

Phase 6 - Check

In this final step the facilitator will guide the group through four checkpoints to ensure that the process is complete and that the group is committed to taking action.

1. Check actions against concerns.
2. Check if the client (the leader) has met their desired outcome.
3. Check all next steps for the group.
4. Check the communication plans.

Facilitation process for this phase:

1. Display list of concerns and action items.

2. Check actions against concerns. Ask for each concern item: "Do any of these action items address this concern?"

3. If the answer is "no" - ask the group if they would like to modify their action item. It's important to do what the group decides. If an action item is modified or a new one created, make sure that it satisfies all criteria.

4. Continue through all concerns on the list in the same manner.

5. Check if the client (the leader) has met their desired outcome.

6. Check all next steps for the group.
    a. Summarize all action items.
    b. Ensure someone is nominated to write up, or save and distribute these to the group and any other key stakeholders and interested parties.
7. Check the communication plans.
    a. Check how the group will communicate their accomplishments and action items.
    b. Ideas include: company website, special pamphlet mailed to employees homes, company newsletter, wall posters in the office, memo or virtual noticeboard, email, information meeting, video or digital presentation, webcast, or via a lunch with key stakeholders, plus many more.

"I think, what has this day brought me, and what have I given it?"

HENRY MOORE

 **Complete Activity # 5**
Facilitation Model

"We have two ears and one mouth so that we can listen twice as much as we speak."

EPICTETUS

ACTIVITY 5: FACILITATION MODEL

Match the Phase with it's definition.

Phase 1 - Identify the Issue	Possible solutions, or possibilities, are the foundation for new and creative approaches to addressing the issue. Open, free thinking brain storming is an easy and highly interactive way for groups to generate numerous innovative answers.
Phase 2 - Concerns	This step focuses on the rationale for determining action steps necessary to address the issue. This step also helps the group explain at a later date their rationale of why (or why not) the group decided on a specific course of action.
Phase 3 - Possible Solutions	In this step the facilitator will guide the group through four checkpoints to ensure that the process is complete and that the group is committed to taking action.
Phase 4 - Criteria	The facilitator needs to clearly identify the topic, concern, issue or problem.
Phase 5 - Action	Its important to gather the concerns from the participants without judgement and without delving into potential negative comments and long-winded discussions.
Phase 6 - Check	Ensure your group takes it's time to work through all Possibilities and Criteria, otherwise double-backing may be required. The final output of this phase is a list of action items in three components: who, what, when.

Activity #5 - check your answers

Check your work from the previous activity.

Phase 1 - Identify the Issue	The facilitator needs to clearly identify the topic, concern, issue or problem.
Phase 2 - Concerns	It is important to gather the concerns from the participants without judgement and without delving into potential negative comments and long-winded discussions.
Phase 3 - Possible Solutions	Possible solutions, or possibilities, are the foundation for new and creative approaches to addressing the issue. Open, free thinking brainstorming is an easy and highly interactive way for groups to generate numerous innovative answers.
Phase 4 - Criteria	This step focuses on the rationale for determining action steps necessary to address the issue. This step also helps the group explain at a later date their rationale of why (or why not) the group decided on a specific course of action.
Phase 5 - Action	Ensure your group takes it's time to work through all Possibilities and Criteria, otherwise double-backing may be required. The final output of this phase is a list of action items in three components: who, what, when.
Phase 6 - Check	In this final step the facilitator will guide the group through four checkpoints to ensure that the process is complete and that the group is committed to taking action.

Now update your Learning Journal (page 85)

QUESTIONS, PARAPHRASING AND SUMMARIZING

Language Patterns

1. Questioning

- **Open ended:** What led you to... discover this / compile that / that decision / this move?
- **Probing:** Will you explain a little more about that?
- **Moving to other participants:** Who has other ideas about this?
- **Encouraging other points of view:** Can anyone provide another point of view about this?
- **Summarizing:** Will someone summarize the points presented so far?

2. Paraphrasing

Paraphrase starters:

- What I heard you say was.... Is that correct?
- I think you said that.... Is that right?
- It seems to me your point of view is.... Is that stated correctly?
- You differ from (Mary) in that you think.... Is that right?

3. Summarizing

Starter phrases for summaries:

- If I understand, you feel this way about the situation.
- There seem to be the following points of view about this.
- We seem to have presented the following issues so far.
- I think we agree on this decision: what we are saying is that we....

"

"If you don't like something change it; if you can't change it, change the way you think about it."

MARY ENGELBREIT

DEALING WITH DIFFICULT SITUATIONS

PART 4

WORKING WITH DIFFICULT ATTENDEES

"If you do not raise your eyes you will think that you are the highest point."

ANTONIO PORCHIA, VOCES, 1943, TRANSLATED FROM SPANISH BY W.S. MERWIN

Ideally, in a discussion all group members participate equally. Rarely does the ideal happen. The term "difficult" is used to indicate group members that either do not participate or have disruptive or controlling behaviors. It is the facilitator's role to encourage active and equal participation, working to keep disruptive or controlling behaviors in check so that they do not prevent the group from completing its task(s).

Understanding Difficult Behaviors

Type of Behavior	Possible Reason	Possible Action of Facilitator
Domineering Controlling	<ul><li>Eager</li><li>Well-informed</li><li>Formal or informal leader</li></ul>	<ul><li>Keep silent.</li><li>Let group respond.</li><li>Recognize contribution and redirect to someone else.</li><li>Avoid looking directly at the person, or giving them direct attention.</li><li>Establish a procedure whereby everyone contributes one idea before group discusses.</li><li>Ask person to summarize ideas so others can contribute.</li></ul>
Argumentative Uncooperative	<ul><li>Combative personality</li><li>Hidden agenda</li><li>Personally upset by some other situation</li><li>Threatened</li><li>Forced participation</li></ul>	<ul><li>Find areas of agreement.</li><li>Direct conversation away from person.</li><li>Let group handle him or her.</li><li>Set and reinforce rule that all ideas are acceptable.</li></ul>
Silent	<ul><li>Timid</li><li>Insecure</li><li>Never given a voice (due to age, gender, social class, ethnic group)</li><li>Thinking about content</li><li>Insecure about language or needing to translate</li><li>Uninterested</li><li>Angry</li><li>Hostile</li></ul>	<ul><li>Encourage with eye contact or invitation to speak.</li><li>Speak to privately to find out what thinking or feeling.</li><li>Use icebreakers to make environment more comfortable.</li><li>Direct questions to this person when he or she has particular expertise or shows non-verbal willingness to speak.</li><li>Allow them time to think and respond</li></ul>
Side conversations	<ul><li>Need to clarify, maybe through translation</li><li>Not interested in discussion</li><li>Culturally appropriate</li></ul>	<ul><li>Set guidelines at beginning of meeting</li><li>Stop meeting and say everyone needs to hear everything</li><li>Address needs for translation beforehand</li><li>Make sure points are clarified throughout discussion</li></ul>

Facilitator Guidelines

Below are some general guidelines for facilitators to keep in mind as they encounter difficult participants:

1. Keep in mind the goal:

- To eliminate or minimize the behavior so that it does not continue to disrupt the group process or isolate some members from participating.

2. Diagnose accurately: take time to think through

- What is the 'problem' behavior?
- Why is it happening?

3. Wait to respond.

- Give yourself time to assess the situation carefully.
- Give the person a chance to change his or her behavior.
- Give the group a chance to control the behavior themselves.

4. Care about everyone in the group.

- Everyone has needs and should be respected.
- Try to address all group members according to what they need.
- Maintain the self-esteem of the person causing the problem by intervening carefully and appropriately.

5. Take appropriate action and follow-up:

- Identify possible alternatives.
- Select best alternative to minimize disruption while maintaining everyone's self esteem.

PROBLEM SOLVING TECHNIQUES — PART 5

REFERENCE: PROBLEM SOLVING TECHNIQUES

"Sticks in a bundle are unbreakable."

KENYAN PROVERB

The following tools create an excellent reference for Facilitators. These problem solving and process improvement tools should be used when the needs of the group require them to analyze and investigate problems. It is important to learn these tools so that regardless of whether you have planned to use the tool or not, you are ready and skilled to use them in a session.

These tools can all be used during in-person or virtual facilitation. They are described as in-person.

The main adaptations for virtual facilitation are to use a virtual whiteboard or collaboration tool with digital notes and annotation/drawing tools.

With a large, more experienced group, consider break-outs to brainstorm initial ideas. Then Facilitator debriefs, collects ideas and continues the process with the whole group.

TOOL #1
BRAINSTORMING

Instructions for using this tool

You will need a large whiteboard or flipchart paper on which to write and a large felt-tipped pen

- The question or issue is written up for all to see.

- Appoint a person as scribe. The scribe must write down every idea as quickly as possible without censoring or qualification (abbreviation is allowed).
  The scribe may also act as the group motivator, constantly calling for new ideas. Alternatively, another person may take the motivator role. The scribe should work in front of the group. All ideas written up must be visible to the whole group.

- Operate with a group of 7-10 people. 15 people is generally the upper workable limit. Try to obtain a mix of people from different backgrounds, divisions, departments and disciplines.

- Have the group define the task in clear terms. Avoid self-limiting definitions. For example, instead of asking "How can we eliminate overtime?", as "How can we improve use of employee work hours?". The later question is more open and will give you more options.

- Ask for crazy ideas early in the brainstorm session. This will stimulate freewheeling ideas which go beyond the established wisdom and known solutions.

TOOL #1
BRAINSTORMING

- There should be no criticism or evaluation of ideas at this stage. If someone disagrees with an idea, or doesn't think it feasible, they should not say so, but should offer an alternative idea (without explanation).

- Seek a large number of ideas. Their quality is irrelevant. Evaluation comes later.

- Link different ideas together. Expand on ideas. Play with them. Encourage the group to be lively - it is a catalyst of creativity.

- Keep the pace fast. Keep comments to a minimum. The scribe should stimulate the group: for example "That's great! Is there any other way we could do it?", "What else could we do?", "How else could it be done?"

- Be aware of the group energy. If the group has run out of ideas, move on to evaluation using the 80:20 rule, fish bone analysis, or any other useful process.

TOOL #2
CAUSE & EFFECT ANALYSIS

This is an analytical technique to map the relationships between cause and effect. It is often called the fishbone technique.

When to use Cause & Effect?

This technique can be used in a wide range of situations to:

- identify the causes of variation for a given problem or desired effect.
- Identify the causes of problems or defects in a process.
- Evaluate the factors which contribute to a negative situation, such as poor staff morale, or poor customer service.
- Map out the complexity of a specific problem or situation.
- Provide an understanding of the inter-related factors that influence a process.
- Provide an understanding of a particular problem, situation or process.

Example of a cause an effect diagram

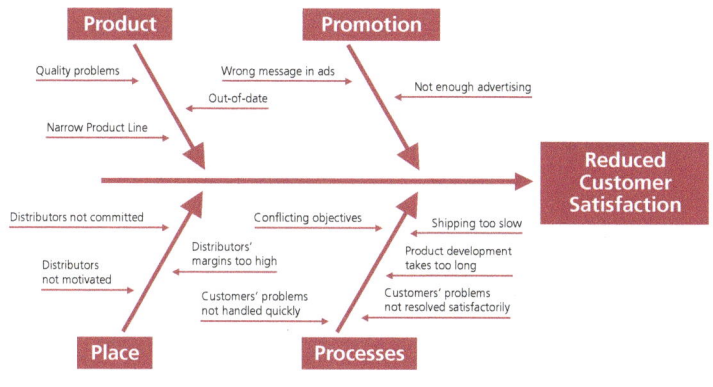

TOOL #2
CAUSE & EFFECT ANALYSIS

How to create a Cause & Effect diagram

- **Decide specifically what effect or problem** you want to analyze: for example high error rates, staff management, communications, quality of service. This becomes the "fish-head". For example:
- **Use brainstorming** to identify:

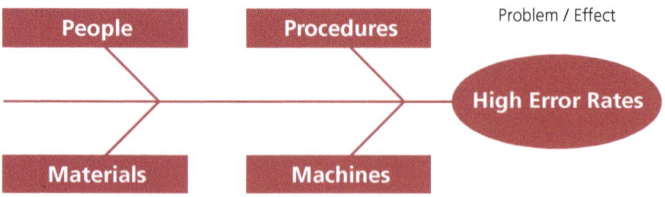

- Causes,
- Components and/or
- Factors that contribute to the effect.
- **Create General Headings.** There are several headings that can be used to stimulate ideas and then categorize them: people, procedures, materials, machines, product, process, promotion, place and so on.
- **Draw fishbone** to graphically place your headings.

- **Decide the relative importance of various causes.** Direct corrective action where it will have most effect.

TOOL #3
USING SMART GOALS

George Doran (1981) has offered a meaningful and easy-to-remember guide for helping us formulate objective statements. His method is called 'SMART'.

Specific	Be specific in targeting an objective.
Measurable	Establish measurable indicator(s) of progress.
Assignable	Make the objective capable of being assigned to someone for completion.
Realistic	State what can realistically be achieved within budgeted time and resources.
Time-related	State when the objective can be achieved, that is, the duration.

TOOL #4
PARETO CHART

Why use it?

To focus efforts on the problems that offers the greatest potential for improvement by showing their relative frequency or size in a descending bar graph.

What does a Pareto Chart do?

- Helps to focus on those causes that will have the greatest impact if solved.

- Based on the proven Pareto principle – 20% of the sources cause 80% of any problem.

- Displays the relative importance of problems in a simple, quickly interpreted, visual format.

- Helps prevent "shifting the problem" where the "solution" removes some causes but worsens others.

- Progress is measured in a highly visible format that provides incentive to push on for more improvement.

TOOL #4
PARETO CHART

How to create a Pareto Chart

Step 1 - decide which problem you want to know more about.

Step 2 - choose the cause or problems that will be monitored, compared, and rank ordered by brainstorming with existing data.

Step 3 - choose the most meaningful unit of measurement – such as frequency or cost.

Step 4 - choose the time period for the study.
- Choose the time period that is long enough to represent the situation.
- Longer studies don't always translate to better information.
- Look for volume and variety in the data.
- Make sure the period of time takes into consideration typical moves (end of month, seasons, different patterns within the week/month).

Step 5 - Collect data either in 'real time' or using 'historical data'.

Step 6 - Compare the frequency or cost of each problem category.
- List problem category, frequency/cost, percentage of total.
- Sort into percentage from highest to lowest.

Step 7 - Create the chart.
- Horizontal axis - categories.
- Vertical axis - values (not %s).

TOOL #4
PARETO CHART

Step 8 – Optional – cumulative percentage line showing the portion of the total that each problem category represents.

- Draw second vertical axis - 0-100% (50% at half way point).
- Draw in cumulative line.

Step 9 - Interpret the results.

- Generally the tallest bars indicate the biggest contributors to the overall problem.
- Dealing with these problems therefore makes common sense.
- Warning: the most frequent or expensive is not always the most 'important'.
- Always ask: "what has the most impact on the goals of our business and customers?"

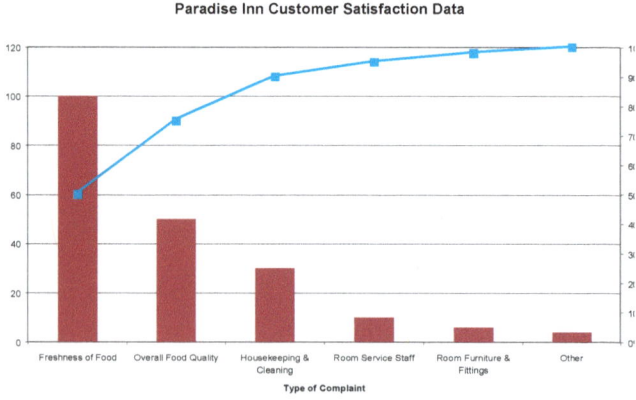

TOOL #5
FLOWCHARTING

Why use it?

- To allow the team to identify the actual flow or sequence of events in a process that any product or service follows.
- Flowcharts can be applied to anything from the travels of an invoice or the flow of materials to the steps of making a sale or servicing a product.

What does a flowchart do?

- Shows unexpected complexity, problem areas, redundancy, unnecessary loops and where simplification or standardization may be possible.
- Compares and contrasts actual versus the ideal flow of a process to identify improvement opportunities.
- Allows a team to come to agreement of steps and examine which activities may impact the process performance.
- Identifies locations where additional data can be collected and investigated.
- Serves as a training aid to understand the complete process.

TOOL #5
FLOWCHARTING

How to create a flowchart

Step 1 - Determine the boundaries of the process
- Where does it start and end?
- Team should agree to the level of detail the flowchart should show.

Macro Flowchart
- Shows only sufficient information to understand the general process flow.

Detailed Flowchart
- Shows every action and decision point.

Step 2 - Determine the steps in the process
- Brainstorm a list of all major activities, inputs, outputs and decisions.
- Use a flipchart paper or digital whiteboard and notes
- Start at the beginning of the process and go to the end.

Step 3 - Sequence the steps
- Arrange the steps in the order they are carried out.
- Use notes so that you can move them around.
- Don't draw the arrows yet.

TOOL #5
FLOWCHARTING

Step 4 – Draw the flowchart using the appropriate symbols

Oval: inputs or outputs
- Inputs: materials, information or actions to start the process.
- Outputs: the results at the end of the process.

Box or rectangle: task or activity in the process
- Multiple arrows can come into a box.
- Only one output or arrow leaves each task box.

Diamond: decision – yes or no answer
- A yes/no question is being asked or a decision is required.
- Yes answers have down arrows from the decision.

Circle with letter or number ID: break in flowchart
- The flowchart is continued elsewhere on the same page or another page.

Arrows: show direction of the flowchart
- Where possible, the flow of the flowchart should go from top to bottom, however left to right is acceptable.

Sample Flowchart

Example – Seafood Process "From Truck to Plate"

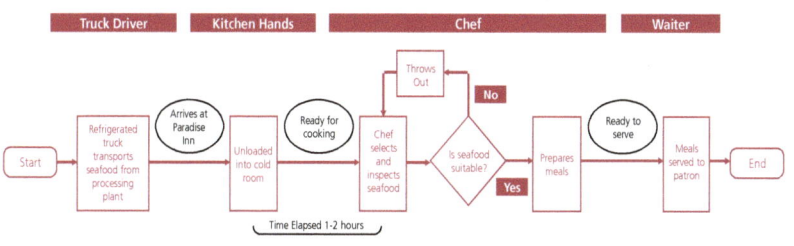

TOOL #6
USING GANTT CHARTS

Overview and History

Gantt Charts were invented by Henry L Gantt and are a special form of bar chart. The Gantt char has horizontal columns. The details of the activities are written down the left-hand axis. These are usually in sequence with the first at the top. The timescale is then shown along the horizontal axis.

Why use Gantt Charts?

One of the benefits of the Gantt chart is that it shows the sequence of activities for easy reference to help manage the project. It could also be used to represent specific requirements, such as project resources.

Milestones can be plotted on the Gantt chart so that actual progress can be measured against the plan.

Computer programs that produce Gantt charts usually incorporate the facility to add dependencies and will then automatically show the critical path.

How to create a Gantt Chart

- List the steps required to complete a project.
- Estimate the time required for each step.
- List the steps down the left side of the chart.
- Write time intervals along the bottom.
- Draw a line across the chart for each step, starting at the planned beginning date and ending on the completion date of that step.

TOOL #6
USING GANTT CHARTS

Some parallel steps can be carried out at the same time with one taking longer than the other; this allows some flexibility about when to start the shorter step, as long as the plan has it finished in time to flow into subsequent steps. This situation can be shown with a dotted line continuing on to the time when the step must be completed.

Example of a Gantt Chart

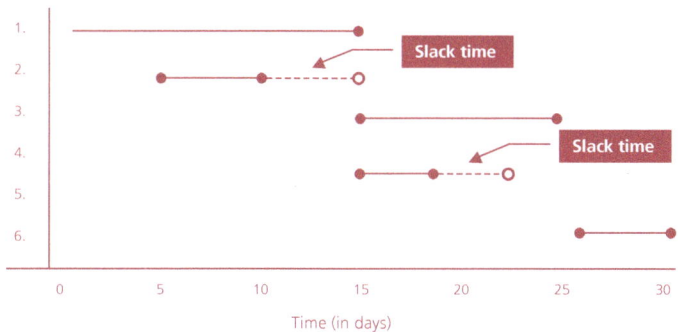

"

"Never doubt that a small group of thoughtful, committed people can change the world. Indeed, it is the only thing that ever has."

MARGARET MEADE

Section 2
LEARNING JOURNAL

The Learning Journal is used throughout the process to record your key learnings, hot tips and things to remember.

Update your Learning Journal at anytime. Ensure you complete your Learning Journal after you finish each activity. Then turn back to the Learning Short-take® to continue your learning.

LEARNING JOURNAL

As you work through this Learning Short-take®, make detailed notes on this page of the lessons you have learned and any useful skill areas. For each lesson or refresher point think about how you could further develop this skill. Your coach will want to discuss these with you in your Skill Development Action Planning meeting.

> *"…that is what learning is.*
> *You suddenly understand something you've understood all your life, but in a new way."*
>
> DORIS LESSING

> *"Act as though it were impossible to fail."*
>
> WINSTON CHURCHILL

> *"The wise do at once what the fool does later."*
> BALTASAR GRACIAN (1601-58), SPANISH JESUIT PRIEST AND AUTHOR.

Learning or Idea	Action to be taken	Result Expected

Learning Journal - continued

Learning or Idea	Action to be taken	Result Expected

> *"Anyone who stops learning is old, whether at twenty or eighty."*
> HENRY FORD

Learning or Idea	Action to be taken	Result Expected

"

*"Do not be too timid and squeamish about your actions. All life is an experiment.
The more experiments you make the better. What if they are a little course, and you may get your coat soiled or torn?
What if you do fail, and get fairly rolled in the dirt once or twice. Up again, you shall never be so afraid of a tumble."*

RALPH WALDO EMERSON

"

Section 3

SKILL DEVELOPMENT ACTION PLAN

Your Skill Development Action Plan is the last Step in the process. After you have completed the Learning Short-take® and all Activities, update your Learning Journal, then complete this section.

SKILL DEVELOPMENT ACTION PLAN

This is the most important part of the program - your individual Skill Development Action Plan.

You need to complete this plan before meeting with your manager or prior to on-going coaching. You will discuss it in detail with your manager or coach as he or she will ensure that you have everything you need to complete the tasks and activities.

Once you have completed your **Skill Development Action Plan** schedule a meeting time with your manager or coach to review your plan. Take your Learning Short-take® and all other documentation received during the training course to this meeting.

Remember - you have committed to your **Skill Development Action Plan**, and need to make time to complete your tasks!

> *"The mind, once stretched by a new idea, never regains its original dimensions."*
> OLIVER WENDELL HOLMES

> *"Whatever you can do or dream you can - begin it. Boldness has genius, power and magic."*
> JOHANN WOLFGANG VON GOETHE

"Imagination is the eye of the soul."
JOSEPH JOUBERT (1754-1824)

Task or activity (Be specific)	Measure (this will help you to know you have achieved it)	Date (Be specific)
Reflect on your Learning Journal. Transfer action items that you can apply to your job. Ensure that you include some 'stretch goals' and also a blend of short, medium and long term goals.	Apart from you, who else is needed to assist you in achieving your goal.	Be specific. A general date such as 'Quarter 1', 'August', or 'by end of year' is vague and more likely to result in not achieving your target. Be specific – e.g. 22nd November.

IDEAS FOR DISCUSSION WITH MY MANAGER

Ideas

CONGRATULATIONS!

You've now completed this Learning Short-take®.

Meet with your Manager/Coach to discuss your
Skill Development Action Plan.

"

"The most important thing in communication is to hear what isn't being said."

PETER F. DRUCKER

"

QUICK REFERENCE

This Quick Reference provides you with a summary of key concepts, models and reference material from Learning Short-takes®. We have also included some quotations to ponder.

Use this section as a quick reference to keep your learning active.

Quick Reference

> **If you do not raise your eyes you will think that you are the highest point.**
>
> Antonio Porchia, Voces, 1943, translated from Spanish by W.S. Merwin

The Skill of Facilitation

Leader-centered:
- Introduce new ideas
- Lead through series of steps
- Test knowledge
- Review activity

Facilitator:
- Help group process own ideas
- Knowledge resides in group
- Manage process, not content
- Encourages all to participate

Traits of an Excellent Facilitator

- Someone who designs work sessions with a specific focus or intent.
- An advisor who brings out the full potential of the work group.
- A provider of processes, tools and techniques that can get work accomplished effectively and efficiently in a group environment.
- A person who keeps a group meeting on track.
- Someone who helps resolve conflict.
- Someone who draws out participation from everyone.
- Someone who organizes the work of a group.
- Someone who makes sure that the goals are met.
- Someone who provides structure to the work of a group.

Preparing a Facilitated Session

1. **Meeting with your Client** to determine the purpose of the facilitation.
2. **Designing the Session.**
3. **Designing the Environment** in which the group will work.
4. **Inviting the Participants.**

Quick Reference

> **The world is round and the place which may seem like the end may also be only the beginning.**
>
> Ivy Baker Priest

Step 1 - Meet with the Client

1. What is the goal?
2. What are the objectives or deliverables of the meeting?

Quick Reference

Step 2 - Design the Session

1. Clarify the **purpose of the meeting**.
2. Define the desired **goals** and **objectives**.
3. Determine **who should attend**.
4. **Design the sequence of meeting activities.**
5. Decide how to begin and how to conclude the session.
6. Determine logistics, equipment and administrative needs.
7. Complete the agenda.
8. Finalize the design with your client.

Step 3 - Design the Environment
The Physical Meeting Room

Atmosphere	Is the room a cheerful color and does it have outside windows?
Layout	Is the room large enough for your needs? Will everyone be able to see the resources you work with and each other?
Furniture	Are the chairs comfortable for longer meetings?
Conveniences	How far away are the rest rooms, lunchroom, elevators, and food?
Lighting	Is there sufficient lighting? Can the room be darkened easily?
Noise	Is the room free of excessive noise and interruptions? Will everyone be able to hear what's going on?
Outlets	Are there enough outlets for equipment?
Heat & Cooling	Will the temperature be appropriate and can you control it yourself?

The Virtual Meeting Room

If the meeting is virtual, choose meeting software that is easy to join, has reliable audio, video and screen sharing capabilities, with all functions and features required for the group to discuss, collaborate and, if necessary, break-out into smaller groups.

Quick Reference

Step 4 - Invite Participants

Nexus Resort ~ Nexus Island ~ South Pacific

Meeting Invitation

To: Chris Tyler, Resort Catering Manager
From: Dan Morrison

Dear Chris,

Our VP of Operations, Lyn Jameson has asked that your work team resolve the problem of increased incidences of food poisoning, suspected as a result of the seafood being served in The Pier restaurant. Lyn has asked me to facilitate a series of problem-solving meetings with you, your team and other key employees of Nexus Resort. Separate invitations have been sent to each of your team members.

The benefits of solving this problem are:
- Reduced or eliminated incidents of food poisoning.
- Identification of the source of the problem.
- Opportunity to revise all processes related to the serving of seafood at the resort.
- Increased customer satisfaction.
- Reduced stress for front-line staff.

We will hold the first meeting at 10:00am on Thursday 4th in the Beachcomber Room in the south wing.

Before the meeting, please review the attached documents and be prepared to brainstorm possible solutions. I will be a neutral facilitator during these sessions and my goal is to help the group identify the required action to solve this problem.

Please call me on my Cell/Mobile number if I can answer any questions regarding the meeting objectives or the facilitation process.

Thanks for helping to solve this problem!
Dan

> **A penny will hide the biggest star in the Universe if you hold it close enough to your eye.**
>
> Samuel Grafton

Quick Reference

Beginning the Session

- **Welcome**
- **Icebreaker** – get the group involved
- **The Agenda**
- Develop **Ground Rules** and **Expectations** for the session

The Facilitation Model

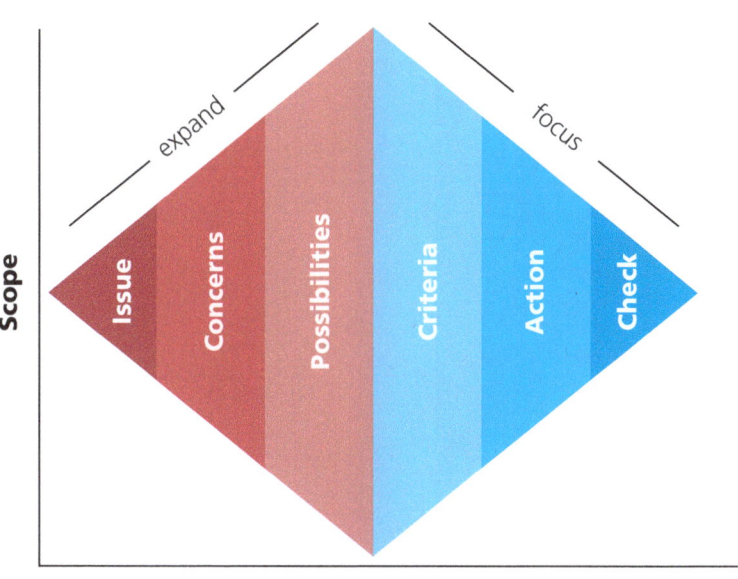

Quick Reference

> **I think in terms of the day's resolutions, not the years.**
>
> Henry Moore

Tool 1: Brainstorming

- The question or issue is written up for all to see.
- Appoint a person as scribe.
- Operate with a group of 7-10 people.
- Have the group define the task in clear terms.
- There should be no criticism or evaluation of ideas at this stage.
- Seek a large number of ideas.
- Link different ideas together.
- Keep the pace fast.
- Be aware of the group energy.

Quick Reference

Tool 2: Cause & Effect Analysis

This is an analytical technique to map the relationships between cause and effect. It is often called the fishbone technique.

Tool 3: Using SMART Goals

Specific	Be specific in targeting an objective.
Measurable	Establish measurable indicator(s) of progress.
Assignable	Make the objective capable of being assigned to someone for completion.
Realistic	State what can realistically be achieved within budgeted time and resources.
Time-related	State when the objective can be achieved, that is, the duration.

Quick Reference

Tool 4: Pareto Chart

- Helps focus on causes that will have the greatest impact if solved.
- Based on the proven Pareto principle – 20% of the sources cause 80% of any problem.
- Displays the relative importance of problems in a simple, quickly interpreted, visual format.
- Always ask: "what has the most impact on the goals of our business and customers."

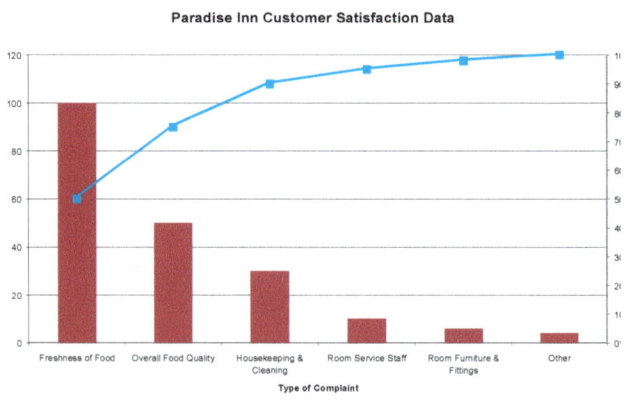

Tool 5: Flowcharting

- Shows unexpected complexity, problem areas, redundancy, unnecessary loops and where simplification or standardization may be possible.
- Compares and contrasts actual versus the ideal flow of a process to identify improvement opportunities.
- Allows a team to come to agreement of steps and examine which activities may impact the process performance.
- Identifies locations where additional data can be collected and investigated.
- Serves as a training aid to understand the complete process.
- A yes/no question is being asked or a decision is required.
- Yes answers have down arrows from the decision.

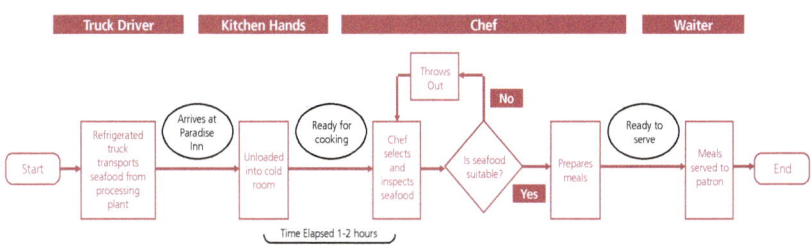

Quick Reference

Tool 6: Using Gantt Charts

One of the benefits of the Gantt chart is that it shows the sequence of activities for easy reference to help manage the project.

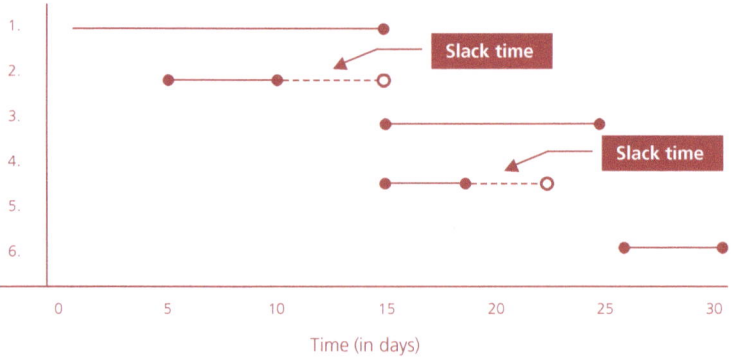

> **People who look through keyholes are apt to get the idea that most things are keyhole shaped.**
>
> — Author Unknown

"
"Gettin' good players is easy. Gettin' 'em to play together is the hard part."

CASEY STENGEL

NEXT STEPS

Congratulations! You have now completed this Learning Short-take® title. The entire list of Learning Short-takes® can be found on the catherinemattiske.com website.

In this section we have suggested Learning Short-take® titles for you that will build your learning. You may order these Learning Short-takes® online at https://www.catherinemattiske.com/books or from your bookstores.

Adult Learning Principles 1
Understanding the Ways Adults Learn

Learning Short-take® Outline

Adult Learning Principles 1 combines self-study with realistic workplace activities for trainers, educators, facilitators and managers to develop skills and knowledge in the principles of adult learning. It will add adult learning techniques to your 'grab bag' of learning design tools for improved learning outcomes. After evaluation of your current approach to learning design, you will learn to develop new and innovative strategies to engage learners at every level. Significantly increasing participant retention and training results **Adult Learning Principles 1** will fuel your confidence in designing successful training workshops and eLearning every time.

The principles of adult learning work on the basis that we all learn differently, and the way we like to receive and interpret information varies from person to person. Trainers and facilitators who use a combination of adult learning principles to provide balance in their programs increase the chances of keeping all participants focused and engaged throughout the learning process. **Adult Learning Principles 1** will assist you in building a good mix of adult learning styles which is critical in ensuring learning, thorough participant retention and workplace application.

Adult Learning Principles 1 includes the job aid Strategies for Meeting Global and Specific Needs, the **Adult Learning Principles Quick Reference Wall Chart** and the **Activity Booklet**, provided as free downloadable tools.

Learning Objectives

- Successfully match adult learning terms with definitions.
- Determine your personal Learning Style preference.
- List and give working examples of three Adult Learning Principles – Global vs Specific, Learning Styles and Learning Types.
- Develop strategies and ideas to link Adult Learning Principles with Instructional Design.

Course Content

- Part 1: Understanding Adult Learners
- Part 2: Adult Learning Principle 1 - Global vs Specific Learners
- Part 3: Adult Learning Principle 2 - Learning Style - Modalities
- Part 4: Adult Learning Principle 3 - Learning Types - The 4Mat System

Making Meetings Work
Getting the Most out of Meetings

Course Content

- Part 1: Types of Meetings
- Part 2: Why Meetings Fail
- Part 3: Solutions to Meeting Barriers
- Part 4: Planning the Meeting
- Part 5: Preparing the Agenda
- Part 6: Conducting the Meeting

Learning Short-take® Outline

Making Meetings Work combines self-study with realistic workplace activities to provide you with the key skills and techniques to make meetings work. Your meetings will become more focused, efficient, targeted and more likely to have a productive impact on the company's bottom-line. You will learn how to more effectively prepare, manage, facilitate and actively participate in meetings.

It is estimated that the average professional spends 61.5 hours per month in meetings, or two weeks every year. It is also estimated that at least 50% of this time is wasted in unproductive meeting activity. **Making Meetings Work** will provide you with the tools to help you save time and money.

Making Meetings Work includes the **Meeting Administration Checklist, Meeting Agenda** and **Meeting Minutes** provided as free downloadable tools.

Learning Objectives

- Evaluate your current level of meeting success.
- Identify the various types of meetings and explain key differences.
- Develop solutions to common meeting problems.
- Outline the steps for a successful meeting.
- Carry out meeting planning and preparation.
- Create a Skill Development Action Plan.

Persuasive Presentation Skills
Create, Prepare and Design with Confidence

Learning Short-take® Outline

Persuasive Presentation Skills combines self-study with realistic workplace activities to provide presenters with the key skills and techniques to prepare and deliver dynamic presentations. After assessing your current approach to preparing and delivering presentations, **Persuasive Presentation Skills** will help you develop unique and innovative strategies to improve your presentation success from small meetings to large audiences. You will learn to effectively plan your communication by using a real-life upcoming presentation.

A dynamic and powerful presentation gives you a platform to communicate your message effectively, influence your audience and spark desired action. Effective presenters spend a considerable amount of time preparing for their presentation, ensuring that the structure, content and communication style is appropriate for their audience. It is often what happens before the presenter gives their presentation that dictates the success of the presentation.

Persuasive Presentation Skills includes the **Persuasive Presentation Skills Presentation Planner**, provided as a free downloadable tool.

Learning Objectives
- Define the importance of preparation in delivering a successful presentation.
- Know how to structure your presentation to deliver key messages.
- Recognize how to connect with your audience and maintain attention.
- Identify key factors for enhancing your message and projecting credibility.
- Design and use visual aids to support your message.
- Describe how to control your nervous energy.
- Create a Skill Development Action Plan.

Course Content
- Part 1: Creating Effective Presentations
  - Overview for Success
- Part 2: Planning Your Presentation
  - 7 Steps for Success
- Part 3: The Presentation Day
  - Reducing Nervousness
  - Tips & Tricks
  - After the Presentation

In Closing...

www.catherinemattiske.com

www.ingramcontent.com/pod-product-compliance
Lightning Source LLC
Chambersburg PA
CBHW042229090526
44587CB00001B/5